National Park Explorers

ROCKY MOUNTAIN

by Lori Dittmer

CREATIVE EDUCATION • CREATIVE PAPERBACKS

TABLE OF CONTENTS

The Rocky Mountains are known for their breathtaking scenery.

WELCOME TO ROCKY MOUNTAIN NATIONAL PARK!

Look at the Rocky Mountains rising above the pine trees! They are capped with snow. Can you see the lakes among the mountains? The Colorado River begins here.

Rocky Mountain National Park is in Colorado. It became a national park in 1915. It is one of the highest national parks in the United States.

★ *Rocky Mountain National Park*
■ *Colorado*

An elk (below); Bear Lake (right)

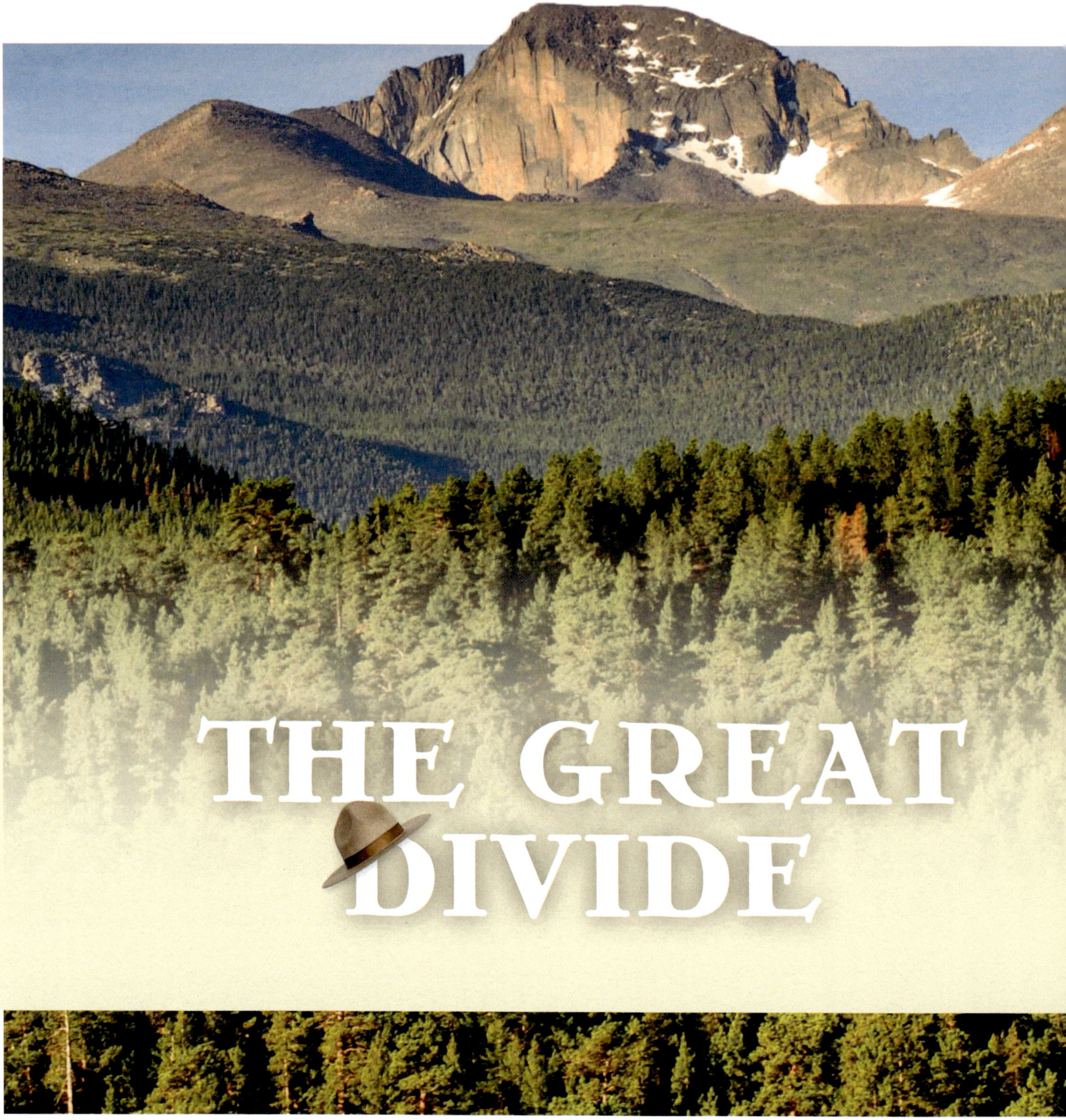

THE GREAT DIVIDE

Longs Peak is the highest point in the park. It is 14,259 feet (4,346 m) tall! The **Continental Divide** runs through the park.

Weather in the Rockies can change quickly. You might see sunny skies, a thunderstorm, and snow all in the same day!

Bighorn sheep (below) can be seen on Flattop Mountain (right).

WILDLIFE ALL AROUND

The growing season is short. Wildflowers fill the meadows with color during summer. Juniper bushes climb the hillsides. They stay green all year.

Bighorn sheep scramble up and down cliffs. Elk **graze** in **alpine** meadows. Yellow-bellied marmots sun themselves on rocks. Bluebirds nest in ponderosa pines.

A marmot (below); a family of bighorn sheep (right)

HEAD TO THE TOP

More than 4.5 million people visit Rocky Mountain National Park each year. There is a lot to do here.

You might find a **waterfall** along a hiking trail. Some people go rock climbing. Others fish in lakes and streams.

A waterfall (below); Colorado Lake (right)

You can drive through the park. Trail Ridge Road is the highest paved **highway** in the U.S. It crosses the Divide. Take your picture next to the sign. You will feel like you are on top of the world!

Snow closes Trail Ridge Road from roughly October through May.

Activity

MINI FOLD MOUNTAINS

Materials needed:
Five or six bath towels of different colors
Two shoeboxes

Step 1: Fold the towels in half and stack them on the floor. This will be the earth's crust. (The crust is Earth's outermost rock layer.)

Step 2: Put a box on each side of the stack. The boxes will be the earth's plates. (Plates are sections of Earth's crust.)

Step 3: Push the boxes toward each other. Watch as the mountains rise. This is how the Rockies formed!

Step 4: Look at the layers of the earth. What do you notice about the colors and shapes?

Glossary

alpine — relating to mountain areas above the tree line

Continental Divide — a natural barrier that prevents rivers on one side from flowing into oceans and seas on the other side

graze — feed on grasses in an open area

highway — a main road, usually connecting towns or cities

waterfall — a place where water flows over a drop in a river or stream

Read More

Herrington, Lisa M. *Rocky Mountain National Park.* New York: Children's Press, 2018.

National Geographic Kids. *National Parks Guide USA Centennial Edition: The Most Amazing Sights, Scenes, and Cool Activities from Coast to Coast!* Washington, D.C.: National Geographic Society, 2016.

Websites

National Geographic Kids: National Parks
https://kids.nationalgeographic.com/explore/nature/national-parks/
Learn about the national parks of the United States, and take a quiz.

National Park Service: Rocky Mountain National Park for Kids
https://www.nps.gov/romo/learn/kidsyouth/index.htm
Read more about this national park, and learn how to become a junior ranger.

Note: Every effort has been made to ensure that the websites listed above are suitable for children, that they have educational value, and that they contain no inappropriate material. However, because of the nature of the Internet, it is impossible to guarantee that these sites will remain active indefinitely or that their contents will not be altered.

Index

Published by Creative Education and Creative Paperbacks
P.O. Box 227, Mankato, Minnesota 56002
Creative Education and Creative Paperbacks are imprints of
The Creative Company
www.thecreativecompany.us

Design by Christine Vanderbeek
Production by Dana Cheit
Art direction by Rita Marshall
Printed in the United States of America

Photographs by Alamy (All Canada Photos, H. Mark Weidman Photography, Robert McGouey/Wildlife, Michele and Tom Grimm, Ron Niebrugge), Dreamstime (Lana Langlois, Ra3rn, Taviphoto, Wisconsinart), Getty Images (Kick Images), iStockphoto (Bkamprath, Gary Gray, JeffGoulden, KenCanning, MRaust, S. Greg Panosian, SeanXu, Sportstock, StevenSchremp, tupungato, Yobab), Shutterstock (Alfie Photography, Tarchyshnik Andrei, Bonnie Taylor Barry, EannClose, Patrick Poendl, MR.Silaphop Pongsai, Josh Schutz)

Library of Congress Cataloging-in-Publication Data
Names: Dittmer, Lori, author. • Title: Rocky Mountain / Lori Dittmer. • Series: National park explorers. • Includes bibliographical references and index. • *Summary*: A young explorer's introduction to Colorado's Rocky Mountain National Park, covering its snow-capped, mountainous landscape, plants, animals such as bighorn sheep, and activities such as rock climbing. • Identifiers: ISBN 978-1-64026-068-9 (hardcover) / ISBN 978-1-62832-656-7 (pbk) / ISBN 978-1-64000-184-8 (eBook) This title has been submitted for CIP processing under LCCN 2018939059.

CCSS: RI.1.1, 2, 3, 4, 5, 6, 7, 10; RI.2.1, 2, 3, 5, 6, 7; RI.3.1, 3, 5, 7; RF.1.1, 3, 4; RF.2.4

First Edition HC 9 8 7 6 5 4 3 2 1
First Edition PBK 9 8 7 6 5 4 3 2 1